LIVING THE PIRATE CODE

Title: Living the Pirate Code

Author(s): Mikazuki Publishing House

ISBN-13: 978-1-937981-01-3 (Print)

Publisher: Mikazuki Publishing House

Copyright: Mikazuki Publishing House. 2013. All Rights Reserved.

The information contained within this book is for educational and commercial purposes and does not necessarily reflect the views of the publisher.

I0176825

LIVING THE PIRATE CODE

TABLE OF CONTENTS

LIVING THE PIRATE CODE

THE PIRATE CODE (Bartholomew Roberts)

I. Every man has a vote in affairs of moment; has equal title to the fresh provisions, or strong liquors, at any time seized, and may use them at pleasure, unless a scarcity makes necessary, for the good of all, to vote a retrenchment.

II. Every man to be called fairly in turn, by list, on board of prizes because, they were on these occasions allowed a shift of clothes: but if they defrauded the company to the value of a dollar in plate, jewels, or money, marooning was their punishment. If the robbery was only betwixt one another, they contented themselves with slitting the ears and nose of him that was guilty, and set him on shore, not in an uninhabited place, but somewhere, where he was sure to encounter hardships.

III. No person to game at cards or dice for money.

IV. The lights and candles to be put out at eight o'clock at night: if any of the crew, after that hour still remained inclined for drinking, they were to do it on the open deck.

LIVING THE PIRATE CODE

V. To keep their peace, pistols, and cutlass clean and fit for service.

VI. No boy or woman to be allowed amongst them. If any man was to be found seducing any of the latter sex, and carried her to sea, disguised, he was to suffer death.

VII. To desert their ship or quarters in battle, was punished with death or marooning.

VIII. No striking one another on board, but every man's quarrels to be ended on shore, at sword and pistol.

IX. No man to talk of breaking up their way of living, till each had shared £1,000. If in order to this, any man should lose a limb, or become a cripple in their service, he was to have 800 dollars, out of the public stock, and for lesser hurts, proportionately.

X. The captain and quartermaster to receive two shares of prize: the master, boatswain, and gunner, one share and a half, and other officers one and a quarter.

LIVING THE PIRATE CODE

XI. The musicians to have rest on the Sabbath Day, only by night, but the other six days and nights, not without special favor.

Source: Bartholomew Roberts Shipboard Articles (1721)

THE ARTICLES OF GEORGE LOWTHER

I. The Captain is to have two full Shares; the Master is to have one share and a half; the Doctor, Mate, Gunner & Boatswain, one Share and a quarter.

LIVING THE PIRATE CODE

II. He that shall be found Guilty of taking up any unlawful Weapon on Board the Privateer, or any Prize, by us taken, so as to strike or abuse one another, in any regard, shall suffer what Punishment the Captain and Majority of the Company shall think fit.

III. He that shall be found Guilty of Cowardice, in the Time of Engagement, shall suffer what punishment the Captain and Majority shall think fit.

IV. If any Gold, Jewels, Silver, &c. be found on Board of any Prizes, to the value of a Piece of Eight ; & the Finder do not deliver it to the Quarter-Master, in the Space of 24 Hours, shall suffer what Punishment the Captain and Majority shall think fit.

V. He that is found guilty of Gaming, or defrauding another to the value of a Shilling, shall suffer what

LIVING THE PIRATE CODE

Punishment the Captain and Majority of the Company shall think fit.

VI. He that shall have the Misfortune to lose a Limb, in time of Engagement, shall have the sum of one hundred and fifty Pounds Sterling, and remain with the Company as long as he shall think fit.

VII. Good Quarters will be given when called for.

VIII. He that sees a Sail first shall have the best Pistol, or Small-Arm, on Board her.

ARTICLES OF CAPTAIN JOHN PHILLIPS

I. Every Man shall obey civil Command; the Captain shall have one full Share and a half of all Prizes; the Master, Carpenter, Boatswain and Gunner shall have one Share and quarter.

LIVING THE PIRATE CODE

II. If any Man shall offer to run away, or keep any Secret from the Company, he shall be marooned with one Bottle of Powder, one Bottle of Water, one small Arm, and Shot.

III. If any Man shall steal any Thing in the Company, or game, to the Value of a Piece of Eight, he shall be marooned or shot.

IV. If any time we shall meet another Marooned that Man shall sign his Articles without the

Consent of our Company, shall suffer such Punishment as the Captain and Company shall think fit.

V. That Man that shall strike another whilst these Articles are in force, shall receive Moses' Law (that is, 40 Stripes lacking one) on the bare Back.

LIVING THE PIRATE CODE

VI. That Man that shall snap his Arms, or smoke Tobacco in the Hold, without a Cap to his Pipe, or carry a Candle lighted without a Lantern, shall suffer the same Punishment as in the former Article.

VII. That Man shall not keep his Arms clean, fit for an Engagement, or neglect his Business, shall be cut off from his Share, and suffer such other Punishment as the Captain and the Company shall think fit.

VIII. If any Man shall lose a Joint in time of an Engagement, shall have 400 Pieces of Eight ; if a Limb, 800.

IX. If at any time you meet with a prudent Woman, that Man that offers to meddle with her, without her Consent, shall suffer present Death.

LIVING THE PIRATE CODE

LIVING THE PIRATE CODE

ARTICLES OF HENRY MORGAN

I. That he should have the hundredth part of all that was gotten to him.

II. That every captain should draw the shares of eight men for the expenses of his ship, besides his own.

III. To the surgeon, beside his pay, two hundred pieces of eight for his chest of medicaments.

IV. To every carpenter, above his salary, one hundred pieces of eight.

V. For the loss of both of the legs, fifteen hundred pieces of eight, or fifteen slaves, the choice is left to the party.

VI. For the loss of both hands, eighteen hundred pieces of eight, or eighteen slaves.

VII. For one leg, whether right or left, six hundred pieces of eight, or six slaves.

LIVING THE PIRATE CODE

VIII. For a hand, as much as for a leg.

IX. And for the loss of an eye, one hundred pieces of eight, or one slave.

X. Lastly, to him that in any battle should signalize himself, either by entering first any castle, or taking down the Spanish colors, and setting up the English, they allotted fifty pieces of eight for a reward.

LIVING THE PIRATE CODE

ANCIENT PIRATES

Ancient pirates in the Mediterranean were so powerful that before Rome emerged as a world power they had managed to sack 400 Roman towns during the last 100 years of the Roman Republic.[i]

In 81 BC, long before his rise to military greatness, Julius Caesar was taken hostage by Cilian pirates. Caesar was on his way to the island of Rhodes where he had intended to study rhetoric from one of the greatest orators of his time.[ii] Near Pharmacussa, Caesar's ship is taken by pirates and the Romans that don't die in the naval battle that followed are taken prisoner. Caesar's ransom is set at 12,000 pieces of gold.[iii] In their book, Outlaws of the Ocean, authors G.O.W. Mueller and Freda Adler mention, "Caesar made his captors listen to his poems and speeches and called them barbarians", for not reacting positively to his performances.[iv]   Caesar let his pirate captors know that there would come a day when he would crucify them all for having kidnapped him. Caesar then has his revenge by waging a naval battle against the Cilian pirates. The pirates that don't perish are taken as prisoners. Caesar then proceeds to crucify them, recovers his gold and takes the ship and booty that his pirate kidnappers had amassed.[v] By the time Julius Caesar was kidnapped by pirates, piracy was ancient as sailing itself. Over 4,000 years ago the Sumerians were already writing about not being able to sail safely because of pirate attacks. The Babylonians outlawed piracy in Hammurabi's Code and put to death any pirate they caught that could not make monetary reparations for their crimes.[vi]

Around the same period of 4,000 BC the Egyptian traders were being raided by Bedouin pirates in the Red Sea. The Egyptians were no strangers to piracy and even sent out pirates of their own to raid Phoenician and Syrian towns like Byblos. Piracy in Ancient Egypt's Nile River Delta grew so out of control that the pharaoh Amenhotep III was forced to set up a type of coast guard to stop pirate attacks. Despite addressing pirate attacks, Amenhotep III was not able to contain piracy on the high seas.[vii]

During the reign of Ramses the II (1292-1225 BC), the pharaoh most know to us because of the story of Exodus in the Bible, piracy in Egypt began to increase significantly. The new cause of the renewed pirate attacks on Ancient Egypt was due to peoples that had been misplaced by encroaching Indo-Europeans. With nowhere to go, the victims of the Indo-Europeans sought out settlement in Egypt but were denied and had no option but to resort to piracy for survival. Ramses II treated these new pirates with an iron fist and killed and enslaved thousands. The Egyptians detested piracy so much that they would punish captured pirates by cutting off their noses.[viii] The success of Ramses II in combating piracy would quite limited. Ramses III would have the honor of vanquishing the pirates that managed to assault Ancient Egypt so successfully. After 1200 BC Egypt was quite successful in ridding itself of much of the piracy caused by the peoples of Greece and Turkey. Ramses the III managed to combat the pirates created by the Indo-Europeans and their settlements on Greek and Turkish lands. The pharaoh used a combination of methods against the pirates in order to come out on top. Ramses III began putting archers on merchant boats as well as setting traps for pirates. The end result of Ramses III's campaign forced the settling of the Sardinian peoples on the island of Sardinia, the settling of the Sikel on Sicily, and sent the Etruscans, that would later greatly influence Roman society, to Italy.[ix]

LIVING THE PIRATE CODE

Further north of Egypt towards the Greek isles lays Crete where a highly developed culture, the Minoans, existed before being wiped out by pirates. From 2000 to 1400 BC Crete was able to flourish commercially because Minoan kings had at their command a navy of ships to deter piracy in their waters. Eventually piracy came to dominate the region and pirates became so powerful that they took over Crete and hastened the downfall of Minoan culture whose settlers had been on the island since 7,000 BC.[x]

The pirates that replaced Minoan society around 1400 BC were of Indo-European descent and they were originally from the areas around the Caspian Sea. They quickly adopted piracy for its high pay offs and because of their fighting prowess. Once established on Crete, the Mycenaean's launched a piratical raid on the city of Troy in Turkey that destroyed the city and formed the basis of Homer's epic the Odyssey.[xi] The Mycenaeans were known to launch piratical raids when they embarked on unsuccessful trading ventures and the profits were usually pocketed by the warriors of Mycenaean nobility. The fear Mycenaean pirates struck on the Ancient Greeks was so great that settlements began to be established away from the coast for increased protection and also in an attempt to stop the highly successful Mycenaean pirates.[xii]

Greek civilization even in its heyday was not free from the scourge of piracy. Piracy was a staple of everyday life in Greece and piracy could generally be found anywhere the Greeks settled.[xiii] The geography of Greece forced many to travel by sea. Most sailors tried to navigate close to land and by doing so they became easy prey for pirates. Not knowing how to read put many more Ancient Greek sailors at the mercy of pirates since safe sailing routes were recorded by mariners in

LIVING THE PIRATE CODE

writings.[xiv] The Ancient Greeks were not merely victims of pirates but also perpetrators of piracy as well. In the mid 460's BC Athenians, which everybody recalls because of their democracy, took control of the island of Scyros close to the Hellespont in order to eradicate piracy in the region simply to replace it with their own.[xv] Greek pirates would also paint their ships to camouflage with the ocean so they were better able to sneak up on their unsuspecting victims. Greek ships were routinely the victims of piracy by the Etruscans and Sicilians. The Greeks were able to subdue Sicilian pirates by sending Greek pirates to the coast of Sicily in order to raid coastal towns. Greek pirates were the first to colonize Sicily and their success later attracted Greek colonist that did not partake in piracy.[xvi]

As the Greek Empire came to an end piracy began to increase and the emerging Romans were forced to officially wage a war on pirates. The

Etruscans also saw themselves forced to settle in mainland Italy to avoid the pirate raids from the west. The Etruscan would later manage to control the seas west of Italy but only with the use of a navy that was made up of pirates.[xvii]

LIVING THE PIRATE CODE

MRS. CHENG – THE GREATEST PIRATE IN HISTORY

The Chinese had no qualms about letting women join pirate crews in the early 1800's. In 1809, one of Mrs. Cheng's battles with the Chinese Navy was raging, Capt. A.G. Course writes, "A pirate wife-they often took part in the fighting-who had been steering one of the junks [as Chinese ships are commonly referred to] defended herself desperately with two swords and wounded several of the naval borders. She gave in only when a musket shot hit her and she fell to the deck." [xviii]

Author of multiple works on pirates David Cordingly mentions of women on Chinese ships, "It was not unusual for women to command the junks and to sail them into battle." [xxix]

Mrs. Cheng fought for the rights of women by stipulating to her pirate crew, "To use violence against any woman or to wed her without permission shall be punished with death." [xx]

LIVING THE PIRATE CODE

Mrs. Cheng entered the world of Chinese piracy in 1801 when she married the pirate commander Cheng I. Before her marriage, Mrs. Cheng earned a living in prostitution in the city of Canton. After 4 years of marriage, the Cheng's and their pirate crews controlled the seas south of China partly through the ransom of captured ships. By attacking fishermen and merchant ships alike Mrs. Cheng and her husband designed a system by which they could live off plundered provisions going ashore only to restock their ships and raid villages.[xxi]

Image of the Hongs, houses of business, held by Western Colonial powers in the city of Canton, where Mrs. Cheng worked briefly as a prostitute.

LIVING THE PIRATE CODE

Mrs. Cheng enjoyed a lot of local support in Chinese villages thanks to the orders she gave her pirates. Cheng's pirates paid for any rice, wine, and other provision because Cheng was known to punish any of her pirates that took these things by force. Thanks to her solidarity, Mrs. Cheng's pirates were always well provisioned but the onslaught of the Chinese government later forced Cheng to change her generous ways.[xxii]

The Dutch Folly Fort on the Canton River where Mrs. Cheng and her pirates launched their attacks.

LIVING THE PIRATE CODE

In 1809, Mrs. Cheng had under her control 1,800 ships and 70,000 male and female pirates. Mrs. Cheng would divide her ships into six squadrons and then assign each one to a geographical area where they would launch pirate attacks. [xxiii] Mrs. Cheng later assigned control of her most powerful pirate fleet to her adoptive son Chang Pao. Mrs. Cheng's son was captured from a fisherman Cheng's husband shortly before his death. Author David Cordingly mentions that, "Within weeks of her husband's death, Mrs. Cheng had also initiated a sexual relationship with Chang Pao, and several years later she married him."[xxiv] The two would later have a son and Mrs. Cheng and her adoptive son remained married until 1822 when Chang Pao died at 36 years of age.[xxv]

Mrs. Cheng and her pirates could be quite cruel despite paying for their basic provisions. Mrs. Cheng was known to have people whipped until they agreed to join her pirate crew or died. Mrs. Cheng's pirates usually killed any people that could not be ransomed but also bought them for $40 from Mrs. Cheng. Once a woman was sold to a pirate Mrs. Cheng expected a pirate to treat his purchase like his wife.[xxvi] If a pirate attempted to abandon the wife or wives purchased from Mrs. Cheng he could be executed.[xxvii] Mrs. Cheng's system for selling captives to her pirates ensured Cheng's profit from the sex lives of all her male pirate crew members. Author David Cordingly mentions of Mrs. Cheng's code of conduct for pirates, "If it was found that the woman had agreed to have sex with her captor [one of Mrs. Cheng's male pirates], the man was beheaded and the woman was thrown overboard with a weight attached to her legs."[xxviii]

LIVING THE PIRATE CODE

Image of an armed Chinese ship with parts labeled from before 1644. From 1808-1810, Mrs. Cheng's pirates began raiding towns and villages and carrying off thousands of people by force to serve as recruits for Cheng's pirate crew. Mrs. Cheng was also known to use her pirates as spies in order to avoid the Chinese Navy.[xxix] Mrs. Cheng was able to defeat seasoned Chinese Navy Admiral Tsuen Mow Sun by encircling Admiral Sun with her superior numbers of pirate ships. In Lantao Island, China Admiral Sun had unsuccessfully attempted to attack Mrs. Cheng and her pirate fleet using burning ships to cause confusion and destruction. Mrs. Cheng was able to win a lot of her battles because of the overwhelming number of ships she commanded but

LIVING THE PIRATE CODE

Cheng's naval strategies should not be overlooked because she was a very astute commander.xxx

Image of a fire ship used by the Chinese Navy from the 1000's.

In her final battle with Admiral Sun, Mrs. Cheng singled out the admiral's ship. Having no escape Admiral Sun committed suicide and Mrs. Cheng was victorious. The Chinese government being completely powerless to stop Mrs. Cheng ordered that no ships go out to sea so that Cheng and her pirates would have no ships to attack. Mrs.

Cheng's pirates simply began using China's multiple rivers to raid towns and decked ships.[xxxi]

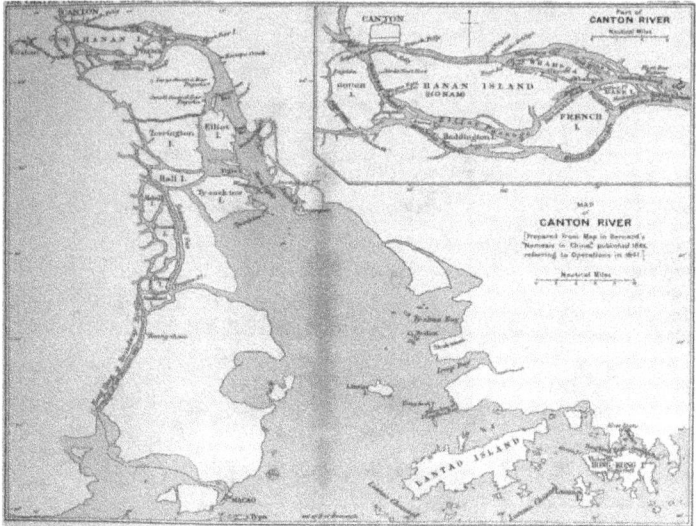

Map from the 1920's showing the Canton River where Mrs. Cheng was known to launch her pirate attacks.

Mrs. Cheng also practiced piracy to take hostages for ransom as was the case of the Englishman Richard Glasspoole and several of his crew members working for the British East India who were later forced to fight for Mrs. Cheng and her pirate crew. Mrs. Cheng used the power of her pirate fleet to extort villages in China and she raided those that did not cooperate. Glasspoole was firsthand witness to the effective cruelty Mrs. Cheng and her pirates could impose since he was forced to raid villages with his captors. Glasspoole mentions that in their first battle against Admiral Tsuen Mow Sun Mrs. Cheng's pirates boarded a Chinese Naval ship where 70 men were cut to pieces and thrown overboard. [xxxii] The Chinese government was unable to stop Mrs. Cheng and her pirates through any military means. In response, the Chinese government was forced to design a plan of pardon that would divide Mrs. Cheng's pirate forces.[xxxiii] Cheng's pirate venture came to an end when her squadron leaders, husband Chang Pao and Po Tae, battled each other and spread discontent to other squadrons.[xxxiv] In 1810, Mrs. Cheng made her way to Canton in the company of 17 unarmed women and children. Mrs. Cheng was fearless in her negotiations with the Chinese government, partly because of the loyalty provided by pirate crew. Chang Pao managed to walk away with the rank of lieutenant, and died a colonel, thanks to Mrs. Cheng's negotiations. Two days after her trip to Canton, 17,318 of Mrs. Cheng's pirates surrendered along with their 226 ships, some of Cheng's pirates were made to pay for their crimes but he majority went unpunished.[xxxv] Mrs. Cheng herself accepted a pardon from the Chinese government but continued to be involved in smuggling. Authors Angus Konstam and Michael Kean write, "[Mrs. Cheng] She died in her 60's, the madam of a well-run brothel in Guangzhou."[xxxvi]

LIVING THE PIRATE CODE

PIRATES FLAGS

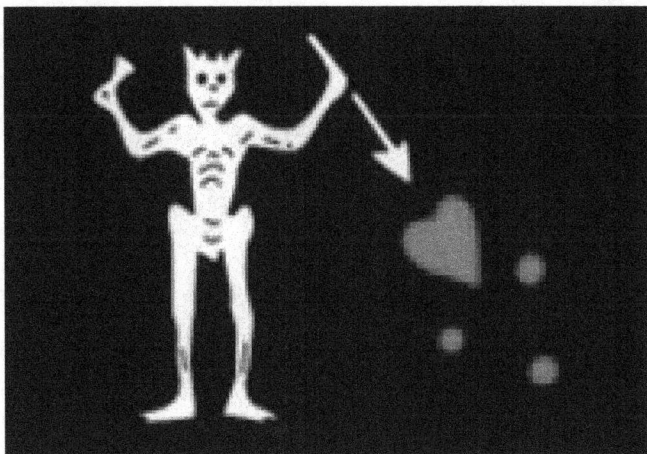

Blackbeard (Edward Teach)

Jack Rackham (Calico Jack)

Bartholomew Roberts (Black Bart)

Stede Bonnet

Thomas Tew

Edward England

Henry Avery

Edward Low

LIVING THE PIRATE CODE

ANNE BONNY

18th Century engraving of Anne Bonny

The notorious female pirate Anne Bonny was the illegitimate child of a lawyer born in Ireland. Anne's birth was apparently the product of an affair between her father and the family maid. Anne's father eventually moved the family to South Carolina where he made a comfortable living as a rice planter. Soon enough, Anne Bonny married but in 1719 she left her husband for Captain John Rackham and his promises of love at sea.[xxxvii] Anne Bonny chose to run away from her husband with Rackham after the pirate captain had failed to buy Anne from her spouse. Anne now faced the prospect of being punished by local courts for adultery which only helped fuel her dreams of being a pirate.[xxxviii] Rackham's crew did not object to Anne joining their pirate crew contrary to the pirate practice of not allowing women on ships. Upon boarding Rackham's ship Anne wore women's clothes but in battle she was known to wear men's attire for increased mobility. Anne Bonny went on to distinguish herself in battle by learning to use Flintlock guns, boarding axes, and swords fearlessly.

LIVING THE PIRATE CODE

The pirate Anne Bonny was not a prudish woman from the 18th Century as we would like to think. Author Frank Sherry writes of Anne Bonny's lust for a captive taken from a Dutch merchant ship, "...Anne revealed herself to the boy, possibly by baring her breasts. In her own way she also made it clear that she felt a strong attraction to the young man. She was amazed, however, when the object of her desire revealed *his* secret: "He" was neither Dutch, nor a man, but a twenty-seven-year-old Englishwoman named Mary Read."[xxxix] Mary Read grew up passing as a boy since her mother had to keep up the facade that Mary was her dead older

LIVING THE PIRATE CODE

brother. Mary joined the military in her adolescence and served in the war Spanish of Succession in Flanders where she met her husband. Soon enough Mary's husband passed away and the family tavern failed forcing Mary to eventually join the Dutch merchant ship. Mary Read adapted quite quickly to the pirate life she was offered by Captain Rackham. Mary's friendship with Anne Bonny eventually led to the jealousy of Captain Rackham but his worries were settled when he learned of Mary's sex during a fit of rage in that he had threatened to kill Mary Read.[xl] Mary Read remained a hopeless romantic and eventually fell in love with an English sailor that had been forced by Captain Rackham to turn pirate. Mary Read would later find herself in a duel with a fellow pirate after her lover was challenged to a duel.

LIVING THE PIRATE CODE

During the Golden Age of Piracy, pirates usually came onto their occupations through joining voluntarily, when captured by other pirates, by mutiny or by desertion from the royal navy. Large shares of pirates were boys who had gone to sea. Desertion in the England's Royal Navy became so common that the Royal Navy kept seamen prisoner on ships for years at a time without allowing them to go ashore. To make matters worse, the Royal Navy had the practice of abducting men to work low paid jobs as sailors. This practice fomented a

LIVING THE PIRATE CODE

great hatred for the Navy on behalf of deserting sailors that became pirates, further attracting people to a life of crime at sea.[xli] In the 1700's, sailors were attracted to the pirate life because there was little opportunity for upward mobility into the post of an officer. Unlike pirates, sailors in the Royal Navy and on merchant ships did not receive an equal share of the profits made from shipping.[xlii]

Piracy becomes lucrative for European nations like England, France, and the Netherlands after the Columbus' expeditions to the New World. Shortly after, English pirates begin assaulting the Spanish coast. The Spanish in the America's treated all foreign ships without permission to trade like pirates. Spanish colonial authorities dealt with foreign traders in a ruthless manner even handing executions.[xliii] The pirate life could be both terrible and rewarding. Pirates valued individual rights to a high degree. Pirates received and equal share of the plunder they acquired. Pirates had and equal vote in choosing whether to fight or evade a ship, where to raid, and how to divide their spoils. Pirate Crews elected their own officers and no special uniforms were worn by the officers. Captains were also chosen through democratic vote and all the pirate crew could make use of the Captain's cabin. The pirate life offered escape from poverty and the freedom to decide one's fate.[xliv] Pirate crews used the position of quartermaster to check the power of a captain because only a quartermaster could decide the appropriate punishment for a pirate crew member that disobeyed orders.[xlv] Pirates were more loyal to their crew than their nations, religious denominations, or race. It was not uncommon to see Americans, Englishman, Frenchman, Spaniards and Portuguese pirates sailing together as pirate crews. The youngest of the infamous Barbarossa pirate Brothers, Hayreddin, employed both a Muslim and Jewish captain for his piratical raids.[xlvi]

LIVING THE PIRATE CODE

Blacks were also accepted as pirates and they usually signed on to flee slavery or because they had been captured on slave ships. Blackbeard's favorite officer was a runaway slave. Author Frank sherry notes, "[The pirate captain] Bartholomew Roberts had more than twenty blacks on his crew".[xlvii] Living aboard a pirate ship was filled with slow days of boredom and plenty of drinking. Pirates were known to eat together and only worked enough to keep their ships running. If a ship became unworthy for sail pirate crews would simply take another ship. Pirates slept where they wanted on a ship and at any time of day or night. Pirate crews were also free to drink all day even on while on duty to quell their boredom at sea. Drinking was seen as fundamental right for these men and alcoholism was a common affliction for pirates. But the love of drinking was so great that Author Frank Sherry mentions, "No captain....ever dared to deny drinking among his crew".[xlviii]

LIVING THE PIRATE CODE

Pirates could be quite good bartenders when they wanted a good drink. They were not particularly picky about what they would drink but their favorite type of alcohol was rum. It was not uncommon for a pirate crew to drink for more than two or three days without end while their ships were anchored ashore. Frank sherry notes two Pirate mixing recipes for a tasty drink, "Pirates mixed rum with white wine, tea, lime juice, sugar, and spices to make a drink they called punch.... They also blended beer, gin, sherry, raw eggs and spices and called it "rumfustian"".[xlix]

While in the heat of battle, just another day at the office for a pirate, it was common to not be able to find a surgeon on a ship so pirates would have a carpenter stand in as one since both professions used the same tools. In his book The Seafarers the Pirates, Author Douglas Botting mentions, "When a man was forced into a pirate crew, he was usually issued a document by the pirate quartermaster certifying that he had been forced; this document could then be used if he were ever out on trial for piracy". Some captured sailors willing to turn pirate would request that they be force to join in front of their officers as a safety precaution, but still most ordinary seaman were executed if brought to trial for piracy.[1]

Pirates knew and practiced their trade well. They would sometimes track a ship for hours and even days while plotting their attacks. Merchant hip crews usually fought to the death because once a battle started with pirates they knew they would not be saved. The practice of walking the plank is largely regarded as a myth. The myth may have come about from the practice of pirates throwing their Roman captives overboard. It is certain though that 17th and 18th century pirates routinely fed their captives to sharks. Once a ship was captured, it was common for 16th century English pirates to display their plunder for sale on their ships.[li]

Upon taking a ship, Pirates had the habit of asking the raided crew if their captain had treated them badly, if so they flogged the captain with tarred rope. Priest and monks were usually victimized because they represented the authority of Spain and Portugal. Pirate crews mocked authority in all its forms and sometimes issued "receipts" to sacked merchants. They also held mock trials when executing captured sailors just for fun.[lii] Pirate crews were not only concerned with plunder and drinking, they were also strict proponents of equality. Madagascar became a pirate haven because of its availability of fresh water and fruits. A lack of warships and a formal government made Madagascar a routine pirate stop.[liii]

This map shows Port Royal prior to the earthquake that sent it under the sea.

In 1664, the Jamaican economy in Port Royal was so dependent on pirates that the governor was forced to stop his attempts at curtailing piracy in the region. The Jamaican pirates of Port Royal fled to the nearby island of Tortuga and Hispaniola which were under French possession. In 1665 the English renewed their aggressions on French, Dutch, and Spanish ships leading to resurgence in piracy.[liv]

HENRY MORGAN

Henry Morgan was one of the buccaneers to roam the Caribbean. Pirates in the West Indies were called so by the French because of their practice of smoking meat in grills made of wood like the natives.[lv]   Captain Henry Morgan was said to have been kidnapped as a child and taken to the West Indies. Morgan finished a sentence for indentured servitude in Barbados before moving to Port Royal and becoming a captain in his 30's[lvi]. In 1665, buccaneer Henry Morgan sacked towns on the Tabasco River in Mexico along with two other English captains. The pirates then made their way south until they reached the poorly defended town of Granada in Nicaragua. Once in Granada Morgan and his entourage took the guns in the city center and reigned hell on the inhabitants of the town. The buccaneers had managed to ally themselves with 1,000 natives.[lvii] In 1668, Captain Morgan sets out sack the town of Puerto Principe in Cuba. In July he reaches Portobello in Panama where he uses captured nuns and friars as human shields. Morgan's strategy works as the governor fires on the members of the religious orders and he manages to take the town. Captain Morgan goes on to collect 100,000 pesos in silver from the town's citizens as ransom when a Spanish army fails to break the pirate's hold on the town.[lviii] Once Morgan received his ransom, he made his way back to Port Royal. The Governor of Jamaica had no option but to tolerate Morgan's actions since the pirate's actions put in motion a state of war between the English and Spanish in the Caribbean. With the blessing of the Jamaican governor, Captain Morgan continued his pirate attacks in Cuba, Venezuela, and the Caribbean. Morgan arrived in Maracaibo in March of 1669, the town was still recovering from two previous attacks from French pirates. The Spanish attempt to inflict the same fate on the English and the begin attacking the north coast of Jamaica with their own pirate raids.[lix]

On December 19, 1670 Morgan arrives on the Chagres River and takes Chagres Castle where he encountered stiff Spanish resistance in his renewed attack in Panama. One of Morgan's men was shot with an arrow, in the heat of battle the victim pulled out the arrow and wrapped it in cotton in order to fire it from his musket. Author Kris E. Lane writes of the event, "By chance....the cotton wrapping caught fire in the muzzle and landed flaming in a thatch roof....setting fire to an ill placed powder keg".[lx] This last feat was enough to change the momentum of the battle and Captain Morgan's pirate crew took the castle. Morgan's crew is harassed incessantly through their trip in Panama

LIVING THE PIRATE CODE

by both the natives and the retreating Spanish soldiers that burned whatever they could find leaving no food for Morgan and his men. At one point the pirates are forced to feed on a group of donkeys.[lxi] Arriving outside Panama City, Morgan's men find the city well defended but decide to fight to death anyway since they have no resources. The Spanish troops find their horses bogged down easily in the mud of Panama's marshes. Captain Morgan renewed his attack for a second day and with the information provided by a captured Spanish officer. With the information obtained Morgan was able to take control of the city in three hours. Captain Morgan's party then occupied the city and sacked all the valuables that could be found. Three weeks of looting Panama were followed by Morgan cheating his crew out of much of the booty collected.[lxii] During his 1671 piracy campaign in Panama, Captain Morgan destroys forts, churches, kills nuns, rapes captive women and tortures boys,

LIVING THE PIRATE CODE

girls and adults in order to have his victims reveal the hiding places of their valuables.[lxiii]

Needless to say Morgan's exploits did not go un-noticed. The Governor of Jamaica was jailed to appease the Spanish. The greater outrage was that Morgan was made governor of Jamaica and General of the West Indies by the English. Morgan's exploits brought to light the necessity for heightened security in the New World which also spelled the end of the buccaneer. Captain Morgan's love for the pirate life never waned and even after his governorship he continued to support buccaneers by allowing them to resell captured ships out of Port Royal. Morgan even continued to issue privateering letters for pirates on Tortuga Island.[lxiv] The English didn't see Henry Morgan as a pirate but simply as a privateer employed legally in the fight against foreign shipping.[lxv] Captain Morgan was eventually knighted and died peacefully in his home in Port Royal in 1688.[lxvi]

Northern Port Royal in 1806.

Alexander Selkirk, the real Robinson Crusoe and the first castaway before Tom Hanks, was rescued by Captain Woodes Rogers. After a grueling expedition that had taken him to the Antarctic, Capt. Rogers and his pirate crew ended up close to the Chilean coast in an attempt to resupply their ship. The pirate crew made its way to the Island of Juan Fernandez, now renamed Robinson Crusoe Island by the Chilean government. Capt. Rogers was forced to steer to the remote island because he was trying to avoid Spanish Colonial authorities. As a formal privateer, Capt. Rogers and his crew would have been executed by the Spanish if caught.[lxvii]

Jack Rackham (Calico Jack)

STEDE BONNET– Former partner of Blackbeard

Stede Bonnet being hanged in Charleston, South Carolina in 1718.

Blackbeard (Edward Teach)

LIVING THE PIRATE CODE

Edward England

LIVING THE PIRATE CODE

Captain Kidd being hanged in Boston Harbor

LIVING THE PIRATE CODE

THE TRIAL OF WILLIAM KIDD

ACTUAL ACCOUNT FROM KIDD'S TRIAL

You stand indicted by the name of William Kidd, late of London, mariner, &c. (And so of the rest.) The jurors for our sovereign lord the king do, upon their oath, present, That William Kidd, late of London, mariner, &c. the 20th day of January, in the 9th year of the reign of our sovereign lord, William the 3rd, by the grace of God of England, Scotland, France, and Ireland king, defender of the faith, &c. by force of arms, &c. upon the high sea, in a certain place, distant about 12 leagues from Callicut in the East Indies, and within the jurisdiction of the Admiralty of England, did piratically and feloniously set upon, board, break, and enter a certain ship, called a Portuguese ship, then being a ship of certain persons (to the jurors aforesaid unknown), and then and there piratically and feloni-ously did make an assault in and upon certain mariners, subjects of the king of Portugal (whose names to the jurors aforesaid are unknown) in the same ship, in the peace of God,

and of our said now sovereign lord the king, then
and there being, piratically and feloniously did put
the aforesaid mariners of the same ship, in the ship
aforesaid then being, in corporal fear of their lives,
then and there in the ship aforesaid, upon the high
sea, in the place aforesaid, distant about 12 leagues
from Calli-cut aforesaid, in the East Indies
aforesaid, and within the jurisdiction aforesaid,
piratically and feloniously did steal, take, and carry
away two chests of opium, of the value of 40Z. of
lawful money of England; 80 bags of rice, of the
value of 121.of lawful money of England; one ton of
bees-wax, of the value of 101 of lawful money of
England; 30 jars of butter, of the value of 10 of
lawful money of England; and half a ton of iron, of
the value of 4 of lawful money of England,
the goods and chattels of certain persons (to the
jurors aforesaid unknown) then and there upon the
high sea aforesaid, in the aforesaid place, distant
about 12 leagues from Calli-cut aforesaid, in the
East Indies aforesaid, and within the jurisdiction
aforesaid, being found in the aforesaid ship in the

custody and possession of the said mariners in the same ship, from the said mariners of the same ship, and from their custody and possession, then and there upon the high sea aforesaid, in the place aforesaid, distant about 12 leagues from Calli-cut afore- said, in the East Indies aforesaid, and within the jurisdiction aforesaid, against the peace of our said now sovereign lord the king, his crown and dignity, &c.

How sayest thou, William Kidd, art thou guilty of the piracy and robbery whereof thou standest indicted, or not guilty?

Kidd: Not guilty.

LIVING THE PIRATE CODE

The Real Robinson Crusoe

When Capt. Rogers and his crew landed on
the Island of Juan Fernandez they found a man
wearing a goat skin yelling back at them in
English.[lxviii] Alexander Selkirk, a native of Scotland,
had been left behind by his former pirate crew on
the ship *Cinque Ports* when he preferred to stay on
the island of Juan Fernandez instead sailing with his
pirate crew on a decomposing ship that later sank.[lxix]
The ship, the *Cinque Ports*, that carried Selkirk to
Juan Fernandez Island was loaded with 10 guns and
was privateering, engaging in sate sponsored piracy,
for Denmark against Spanish ships.[lxx] Alexander
Selkirk made the best of four and a half years on the
island by surviving off of goat herds left behind by
Spaniards. Selkirk had used goat skins to clothe and
shelter himself with. By the time of his rescue
Selkirk had constructed 2 tents made of goat skins.
He was forced to domesticate some cats he had

found on the island to keep rats from nibbling at his toes. Spaniards had visited the island while Selkirk was confined to it and he was forced to hide in a tree while one of the Spaniards urinated under it. Selkirk could not allow himself to be seen much less recued by Spaniards for if caught Selkirk would have been executed as pirate by the Spanish for having been a part of a privateering expedition.[lxxi] The pirate crew of the *Cinque Ports* which had abandoned Selkirk on Juan Fernandez Island later had their ship sunk from the terrible state it was in and 70 of the ship's survivors were jailed in Peru all while Selkirk was being rescued.[lxxii]

All the years spent on the Island of Juan Fernandez caused Selkirk's feet to callus from a lack of shoes. Days after the landing of Capt. Rogers and his pirate crew on the island Selkirk recognized one of the officers [William Dampier] that had commanded the failed privateering expedition that landed Selkirk on Juan Fernandez. Selkirk refused to be rescued even preferring to stay on the island until Capt. Woodes Rogers and his crew reassured Selkirk that Dampier was not in charge of Rogers' privateering mission. Selkirk then helped to provision Capt. Rogers' vessels and sailed off into the pages of popular literature by inspiring Daniel Defoe to write Robinson Crusoe. Selkirk continued to sail with Capt. Rogers and the two men continued their piracy expeditions against Spanish ships.[lxxiii]

STEDE BONNET

The Major was a Gentleman of good Reputation in the Island of Barbados, was Master of a plentiful Fortune, and had the advantage of a liberal Education. He had the least temptation of any man to follow such a life, from the condition of his circumstances. It was very surprising to everyone, to hear of the Major's enterprise, in the

LIVING THE PIRATE CODE

island where he lived and as he was generally esteemed and honored, before he broke out into open Acts of Piracy, for he was afterwards rather pitied than condemned, by those that were acquainted with him, believing that this humor of going pirating, proceeded from a disorder in his mind, some Time before this wicked undertaking, and which is said to have been occasioned by some discomforts he found in a married state. Be that as it will, the Major was but ill qualified as he had no understanding of maritime affairs. However, he fitted out a sloop with ten guns and 70 men, entirely at his own expense, and in the night-time fitted from Barbados. He called his sloop the Revenge; his first cruise was off the coast of Virginia where he took several ships and plundered them of their provisions, cloth, money, and ammunition. They took Captain Montgomery and the Pirate Crew set the ship on fire. From here they went off the East End of Long Island and took a

Sloop bound for the West Indies, after which they landed some men at Gardner s Island in a peaceable manner. They bought provisions for the company's use, which they paid for, and so went off again without molestation. Sometime after, which was in August 1717, Bonnet came off the South Carolina and took a sloop and a Brigantine bound in the sloop laden with rum, sugar and Black slaves. The Brigantine they plundered, and then dismissed, but they sailed away with the sloop, and at an inlet in North Carolina, careened her and set her on fire. After the Sloop had cleaned, they put to Sea, but came to no resolution what course to take, the crew were divided in their opinions, some being for one thing and some another. Nothing but confusion seemed to attend all their schemes. The Major was no sailor as was said before, and therefore had been obliged to yield to many things that were imposed on him, during their undertaking, for want of a competent knowledge in maritime affairs. Finally, the Major Bonnet fell in company with another Pirate, an Edward Teach (who because of his remarkable black ugly beard, was more commonly called Black-Beard). Black-Beard was a good sailor, but a most cruel hardened villain, bold and daring to the last degree, and would use it for perpetrating the most abominable wickedest imaginable acts for which he was made chief of that gang. Black-Beard being truly the superior in roguery, of all the Company, as has been already related.

To Black-Beard, Bonnet's Crew joined in happiness and Bonnet himself had, notwithstanding the Sloop was his own. He went aboard Black-Beard's ship, not concerning himself with any of their affairs, where he continued till one Richards was appointed Captain of Bonnet's ship in his Room. The Major now saw his folly, but could not help himself, which made him melancholy and was confounded with shame, when he thought upon what he had done. His behavior was taken notice of this by the other pirates, who liked him never the better for it. Bonnet declared to them, that he would gladly leave off that way of living, being fully tired of it, but he was ashamed to see the face of any English man again. Therefore if he could get to Spain or Portugal where he might be undiscovered, he would spend the remainder of his days in either of those countries, otherwise he must continue with them as long as he lived.

When Blackbeard lost his ship and surrendered to the King's Proclamation, Bonnet re-took command of his own Sloop Revenge, and sailed away to North Carolina. The War had broken out between the Triple Allies and Spain, therefore Major Bonnet got a clearance for his sloop at North Carolina to go to the island of St. Thomas with a plan to get the Emperor's Commission to go privateering upon the Spaniards. Privateers were essentially pirates that had the full blessing and support of their nation in the form of a Commission granted to them to attack enemies. When Bonnet came back to the Revenge, he found that Teach and his gang were gone, and that they had taken all the money, small arms and everything of value out of the great ship, and set ashore on a small sandy island. Seventeen men remained with an understanding that they would perish because there were no inhabitants or provisions nor any boat or materials to build or make any kind of launch or vessel, to escape from that desolate place. They remained there two nights and one day without food, expecting nothing else but a lingering death. Major Bonnet received information about them being there, by two of the pirates who had escaped Teach's cruelty. Major Bonnet sent his boat to make discovery of the truth of the matter, which the poor wretches seeing, made a signal to them, and they were all brought on board Bonnet's sloop. Major Bonnet told all his

Company, that he would take a Commission to go to St. Thomas, therefore if they would go with him they should be welcome, whereupon they all consented. But as the sloop was preparing to sail, a boat that brought apples and cider to sell to the sloop's men informed them of Captain Teach's location and that he had only 18 or 20 men with him. Bonnet who bore him a mortal hatred for some insults offered him, went immediately in pursuit of Teach, but it happened too late, and after four days cruise, hearing no further news of him, they steered their course towards Virginia. Two days afterwards they chased a Sloop of fifty tons, and took her as to get a supply of liquor. They brought from her rum, which it seems they had need of, though they had not ready money to purchase them. What security they intended to give is unknown, but Bonnet sent eight men to take care of the prize sloop, who perhaps, not caring to make use of those accustomed freedoms, took the opportunity to go off with the ship. Bonnet who was pleased to have himself called Captain Thomas, saw them no more.

After this, the Major threw off all restraint, and though he had just before received his Majesty's Mercy in the name of Stede Bonnet, he relapsed in good earnest into his old vocation, by using the name of Captain Thomas. Bonnet recommenced being a pirate by taking and plundering all the vessels he met with. He took off Cape Henry two Ships from Virginia bound to Glascony, out of which they had very little besides a hundred weight of tobacco. The next day they took a small sloop bound from Virginia with twenty barrels of pork, some bacon, and they gave her in return, two barrels of rice and other victuals. The next they took was another Virginia man, out of which they had nothing of value, only a few combs, pins and needles, and gave her instead thereof, a Barrel of

LIVING THE PIRATE CODE

pork, and two barrels of bread. From Virginia they sailed to Philadelphia and in the Latitude of 38 North, they took a scooner coming from North Carolina, with two dozen calf-skins to make covers for guns, and two of their hands, and detained her some says. All this was but small game, and seemed as if they planned only to make provision for their sloop until they arrived at St. Thomas. They hitherto had dealt favorably with all that were unhappy as to falling to their hands, but those that came after, fared not too well. They took a sloop of fifty tons bound from Philadelphia to Barbados. The last day of July, they took another sloop of 60 tons, bound from Antigua to Philadelphia, which they likewise kept with all the cargo, consisting chiefly of rum, molasses, sugar, cotton, indigo, and about 2 Pounds in money, valued in all at 500 Pounds. Upon the information of Major Bonnet's activity, the Council of South Carolina was alarmed, and apprehensive that they should receive another visit from them. Colonel William Rhet of Province waited on the Governor, and offered himself to go with two Sloops to attack this pirate, which the Governor readily accepted, and accordingly gave the Colonel a Commission and full power to fit such vessel as he thought proper for this plan. In a few Days two Sloops were equipped and manned: The Henry with 8 Guns and 70 Men, and the second ship with 8 Guns and 60 Men, both under the entire direction and command of the aforesaid Colonel Rhet. On the14th of September, the Colonel went on board the Henry and with the other sloop, sailed from Charlestown to prepare for the cruise. Just then arrived a small ship from Antigua with an account that he was taken and plundered by one Charles Vane, a pirate in a Brigantine of 12 Guns and 90 Men. Charles Vane had also taken two other vessels bound in there, one a small Sloop, the other a Brigantine. This proved fortunate to the owners for Teats having often

LIVING THE PIRATE CODE

attempted to quit this course of life, took an opportunity in the night to leave to the south of Charlestown and surrendered to his Majesty's pardon. The owners got their Negroes, and Teats and his men had certificates given them from the Government. Vane cruised some time in hopes to catch Teats and unfortunately for them, took two Ships coming out, bound to London and while the prisoners were aboard, some of the pirates gave out, that they planned to go into one of the rivers to the South. Colonel Rhet upon hearing this, sailed over with the two sloops before mentioned and having the wind northerly, went after the pirate Vane and scoured the rivers and inlets to the southward, but not meeting with him, tacked and flood for Cape Fear River, in prosecution of his first design. On the 26th following, in the evening, the Colonel with his small squadron, entered the river, and law, over a point of land, three sloops at an anchor, which were Major Bonnet and his prizes; but it happened that in going up the River, the pilot run the Colonel's sloops aground, and it was dark before they were on float, which hindered their getting up that night. The pirates soon discovered the sloops, but not knowing who they were or upon what design, they came into that river, manned three canoes, and sent them down to take them, but they quickly found their mistake, and returned to the sloop, with the unwelcome news. Major Bonnet made preparations that night for engaging, and took all the men out of the prizes. He showed one of his prisoners a letter he had just wrote, which he declared he would send to the Governor of South Carolina.

The letter was to this effect:

That if the sloops, which then prepared, were sent out against thirty by the aid of the Governor and he should get clear of that he would burn and destroy all Ships going or coming out of South Carolina.

LIVING THE PIRATE CODE

The next morning they got under sail, and came down the river, planning only a running fight. Colonel Rhet's sloops got likewise under sail and stood for him, getting upon each quarter of the pirate, with intent to board him, which he perceiving, edged in towards the shore, and being warmly engaged, their sloop ran aground. The Carolina Sloops being in the same shoal water, were same circumstances. The Henry, in which Colonel Rhet was grounded within pistol shot of the pirate, and on his bow the other sloop grounded right ahead of him, and almost out of gunshot, which made her of little service to the Colonel, while they lay aground.

At this time the pirate had a considerable advantage for their sloop after she was aground, lifted from Colonel Rhet by which means they were all covered, and the Colonel's sloop lifting the same way, his men were much exposed not-withstanding which, they kept a brisk fire the whole time they lay thus aground, which was near five hours. The pirates made a bloody flag and beckoned several times with their hats to the Colonel's men, to come on board, which they answered with cheerful hurrah's and said, that they would speak with them by and by ; which accordingly happened, for the Colonel's Sloop being first a float, he got into deeper water, and after mending the sloop's rigging, which was much shattered in the engagement, they stood for the pirate, to give the finishing stroke to go directly on board with him which he prevented by sending a flag of truce. After some time capitulating, they surrendered themselves prisoners. The Colonel took hold of the sloop, and was extremely pleased to find that Captain Thomas who commanded her, was the individual person of Major Stede Bonnet who had done them the honor several times to visit their own coast of Carolina.

LIVING THE PIRATE CODE

There were killed in this action on board; the
Henry lost ten men, and had fourteen wounded and
on board the other sloop, the Sea Nymphy, two
were killed and four wounded. The Officers and
Sailors in both sloops behaved themselves with the
greatest bravery and had not they unluckily run
aground, they would have taken the pirates with
much less loss of men, but as he designed to get by
them, and so make a running fight, the Carolina
sloops were obliged to keep near him, to prevent his
getting away. Of the pirates there, seven were killed
and five were wounded, two of which died soon
after from their wounds. Colonel Rhet weighed the
30th of September from Cape Fear River, and
arrived at Charlestown to the great joy of the whole
Province of Carolina. Bonnet and his crew, two
days after were put ashore, and there not being a
public prison, the pirates were kept at the Watch
House, under a Guard of Militia but Major Bonnet
was committed into the custody of the Marshal, at

his house and in a few days after, David Harlot the
Mailer and Ignatius Tell the Boatswain, who were
going to provide evidence against the other pirates,
were removed from the rest of the Crew, to the said
Marshal's house, and every night two sentinels set
about the said house. But whether through any
corruption or negligence in guarding the prisoners,
on the 24th of October the Major and Harlot made
their escape, the boatswain refusing to go along
with them. This made a great noise in the province,
and people were open in their resentments, often
reflecting on the Governor and others in the
Magistracy, as though they had been bribed for
conniving at their escape. These invectives arose
from their fears that Bonnet would be capable of
raising another Company, and prosecute his
revenge against this Country, for what he had lately
suffered : But they were in a short time made easy
in those respects, for as soon as the Governor had
the account of Bonnet's escape, he immediately

LIVING THE PIRATE CODE

issued out a proclamation, and promised a reward of 700 Pounds to any that would take him, and sent several boats with armed men, both to the north and south, in pursuit of him. Bonnet sailed to the north in a small vessel, but wanting necessaries including food, water, and ammunition, and the weather being bad, he was forced back. He returned with his canoe to an island near Charlestown to fetch supplies but there being some information sent to the Governor, he sent for Colonel Rhet and asked him to go in pursuit of Bonnet and accordingly gave him a Commission for that purpose. Wherefore the Colonel, with proper craft, and some Men, went away that night for the island and after a very diligent search discovered Bonnet and Harlot together. The Colonel's men fired upon them and killed Harlot upon the spot, and wounded one Negro and an Indian. Bonnet submitted, and surrendered himself, and the next morning, being November the 6th, was brought by Colonel Rhet to

LIVING THE PIRATE CODE

Charles-Town. By the Governor's Warrant, he was taken at last in to custody, in order for his being brought to his trial. On the 28th of October 1718, a Court of Vice Admiralty was held at Charles-Town in South Carolina and by several Adjournments, continued to Wednesday the 12th of November. The trial of the pirates taken in a sloop formerly called the Revenge was tried before Nicholas Troty Esq., Judge of the Vice-Admiralty and Chief Justice of the said Province of South Carolina and other Assistant Judges. The King's Commission to Judge Trot was read and a Grand Jury sworn for the finding of the several Bills, and a learned Charge given them that had been issued by the Judge. The indictments being found, a petit Jury was sworn, and the pirates arraigned and tried. All, except four were found guilty and received sentences of death. Most of them were tried upon two indictments as follows:

LIVING THE PIRATE CODE

THE Jurors for our Sovereign Lord the King do on their Oath present that Stede Bonnet on the day of August, in the fifth year of the reign of our Sovereign Lord George, by force of arms upon the high sea in a certain place called Cape James, did piratically and feloniously set upon board and entered a certain merchant sloops called the Frances, by forces upon the high sea in a certain place called Cape James, about two miles from the shore or thereabouts and within the jurisdiction of the Court of Vice-Admiralty of South Carolina. Being a sloop, it piratically and feloniously did make an assault upon the said ship against the peace of God, and of our said now Sovereign Lord the King. theny and there being piratically and feloniously did put the aforesaid ship captains and others in the Sloop, them being in corporal fear of their lives. Then and there, in the sloop aforesaid upon the High-Sea, in the place aforesaid called Cape James.

LIVING THE PIRATE CODE

This was the form of the indictments they were arraigned upon, and though they might have proved several more facts upon the major part of the crew, the Court thought fit to prosecute but two •f the others was for acting in a piratical and felonious Manner. All the prisoners arraigned pleaded Not Guilty, and put themselves upon their trials, except James Wilson and John Levity who pleaded Guilty to both indictments and Daniel Perry, to one only. The Major would have gone through both indictments at once, which the Court not admitting, he pleaded Not Guilty to both indictments, but being convicted of one, he retracted his former plea to the second Indictment, and pleaded Guilty to it. The prisoners made little or no defense, every one pretending only that they were taken off a marooned shore, and were shipped with Major Bonnet to go to St. Thomas. But being out at sea and wanting provisions, they were obliged to do what they did by others. So did Major Bonnet himself, pretend that it was by force and not inclination that occasioned what had happened. However, the facts being plainly proved, and that they had all shared ten or eleven Pounds a Man, excepting the three last, and Thomas Nichols they were all but three, found Guilty. The Judge made a very grave Speech to them, setting forth the severity of their crimes yet the condition they were now in and the nature and necessity of an unfeigned repentance and then recommended them to the Ministers of the Province, for more ample directions to fit them for eternity, for concluded he that the priest's lips shall keep knowledge and you shall "seek the law at their mouths" for they are the messengers of the Lord. Then he pronounced the sentence of death upon them. On Saturday November the 8th, 1711. Robert Tucker, Edward Robinson, Neal Paterson, William Scot, Job Bayley, John William Smith, John Thomas, William

LIVING THE PIRATE CODE

Morrison, Samuel Booth, William Hewit, William Eddy, Alexander Annand, George Ross, George Dunlin, Matthew King, Daniel Terry, Henry Virgin, James Robbins, James Mullet, alias Millet, Thomas Trice, John Lopez, and Zachariah Long, were executed at the White-Point near Charlestown, pursuant to their sentence. As for the Captain, his escape protracted his fate, and spun out his life a few days longer for he was tried the both, and being found Guilty, received sentence in like manner as the former before which Judge Trot made a most excellent speech to him, rather somewhat too long to be taken into our history.

LIVING THE PIRATE CODE

The Lord Chief Justice's speech upon his
pronouncing sentence on Major Stede Bonnet:

*Major Stede Bonnet you stand here convicted upon two
indictments of piracy, one by the Verdict of the Jury, and
the other by your own confession. Although you were
indicted but for two facts, yet you know that at your
trial it was fully proved even by an unwilling witness,
that you piratically took and rifled no less than thirteen
vessels, that you sailed from North-Carolina. So that
you might have committed eleven more acts of piracy,
you took the benefit of the King's Good Grace and
pretended to leave that wicked course of life. Not to
mention the many acts of piracy you committed before,
for which if your Pardon from Man was never
authentic yet you must expect to answer for them before
God. You know that the crimes you have committed are
evil in themselves and contrary to the Light and Law of
Nature as well as the Law of God, by which you are
commanded that you shall not steal.*

But to theft you have added a greater Sin, which is murder. How many you may have killed of those that resisted you in the committing your former piracy, I know not. But this we all know. That besides the wounded, you killed no less than eighteen persons out of those that were sent by lawful Authority to suppress you, and just a stop to those rapines that you daily added. And however you may fancy that that was killing men fairly in open fight, yet this know, that the power of the Sword-not being committed into your hands by any lawful authority, you were not empowered to use any Force, or fight anyone; and therefore those persons that fell in that action, in doing their duty to their King and Country, were murdered, and their Blood now cries out for vengeance and justice against you: For it is confirmed by the Law of God, that whosoever sheddeth man's blood by man shall his blood he shed.

LIVING THE PIRATE CODE

PERSIAN GULF PIRATES

The following is an article that was published in the New York Times in 1867:

To the Editor of the Chicago Tribune: Abraham Moosa is now proprietor of a stall in the Bazaar of Muscat, and when last I saw him was doing a good business in pearls. Ten years ago you would have found him a wandering Bedouin some-where on the plains between Oman and Hadramaut. His mother was the fifth wife of DOOLA MOOSA MOOSA, and as such she shared the fortunes of one of the greatest villains the world ever produced. DOOLA MOOSA MOOSA and his clique, numbering some 500 Bedouins, formed a tribe the most terrible of pirates that infested the Persian Gulf and its adjacent waters. D. M. Moosa & Co., flourished for nearly a quarter of a century until the British gun-boat Tiger put an untimely end to the firm in the year 1848. Their retreat, a strong one' was found out, and the Tiger captured forty craft besides four large armed buglahs, each carrying from fifteen to twenty guns, six and nine-pounders. In the hold of one, the Sheikh El Emir, there was collected together no less than thirty-two pairs of skeleton hands. many skulls, beside odd mile, legs and other parts of the human body. The pirates fought like demons, but were in time beaten; few were taken prisoners, and far too many were allowed to escape under the fastness of the mountains. Twelve years after this event I had the pleasure of being stationed in the precise locality of the above occurrence—at Elphinstone's Inlet, a spa some twelve miles distant, west of Cape Mussendon, on the eastern coast of Arabia. My business at this place was to endeavor, in making arrangements with the neighboring sheiks of the Bedouins, to guarantee that none of their people would amuse themselves by cutting the throats of the telegraphists who were about to locate in that neighborhood. It was here I met Abraham Moosa, and finding him somewhat of a civilized being, employed him as my moonshe (secretary) and interpreter. One Tuesday night he became very much excited. It was the anniversary of the death of his father, "who was brutally murdered just there," said MOOSA, pointing over his left shoulder into the intense darkness of the night. I was alone and felt uncomfortable. The Government of Bombay had provided for my reception a hulk and a crew of Hindoos. This hull was moored fore and aft, and to me it always appeared singularly suggestive of a floating target on which the settling Arabs of the shore could practice with excellent convenience to themselves. It by a halt a mile, either end, from a wall some hundred feet high, of black, gaunt and inhospitable rocks. Covering the tops of these hills pretty thickly were the worst breed of Bedouin—" a man who never says his prayers." Among the multiplicity of orders the Bombay Government gave me, when leaving, was one most particularly to find out, at any cost or expense, what had become of a boat's crew numbering eighteen hands who had left their vessel in search of fresh water, and had never been heard of afterward. The ship to which they belonged was named the Constance, trading between America, Muscat and Calcutta. I began talking over the matter with Moosa that very Tuesday night, and finished about 4 o'clock the next morning. 'The arrangement was almost complete. MOOSA agreed to tell me the whole of the story, and I in return promised him one thousand rupees, and so set him up in an honest trade. He was tired of the Bedouin life. He had cut many throats; he had forgotten how many; he was tired of counting when he got over the fiftieth. The money was paid. I obtained it from a Jew of Kilshain. I heard the tale, and here it is from my diary as told by MOOSA. The crew landed, leaving two men to mind the beat on the beach. The guide who were to take them to the wells led them into a mountain pass; they were surrounded by hundreds of the Bedouins. It was only a month past since a gunboat had caught and hanged eighteen of this piratical gang, so now came the Arab revenge. Some of the crew were killed on the spot: the remainder, about twelve in number, were dragged into the hills; a Bedouin Court sat and tried the prisoners, and the crew were then one by one tied to pieces of projecting rock and "jambiered," which is no more or less than hacking pieces of muscle from their bodies. This occurred about noon, and they were then left to bleach and perish in the sun. So they died most assuredly the worst kind of agonizing deaths. I sent a special messenger to Bombay, and in the course of a month I had the British gunboat Vigilant with me to investigate the matter. The spot in the mountains was accurately described to us by Moosa and we found it with little difficulty. On landing, we passed through the settlement of the

Bedouins, who offered to join us "for our safety," as they expressed it. On our return they had decamped. Beside some pieces of rocks we found all we wanted, the remains of nine or ten men. These were collected together in a sack, which we carried away, to, give a decent burial. A little island some distance off we selected and it is now marked in all good maps as the tombs.

Source: The New York Times

LIVING THE PIRATE CODE

MODERN PIRATES

Piracy may seem like an issue of the past but the trade continues to be a profitable one for anyone daring enough to seek it out. Our modern times are not safe from piracy on the high seas because the vastness of Earth's oceans. This reality prevents even the largest of navies, coast patrols, or sovereign nations from being able to effectively police the world's oceans. In addition, the modern shipping industry is composed of 50,000 commercial ships and 1,000,000+ employees serving as sailors. There are three main conditions that drive piracy in our times; lack of a strong central government with enough resources to police the seas bordering a nation, active commercial shipping lanes, and poverty.[lxxiv]

Modern-day piracy began to increase shortly after World War II. Piracy mainly affected African and Asian countries many of which had managed to secure independence from European colonies. The nations created in Africa and Asia simply didn't have the money to invest in functioning navies or coastal patrols.[lxxv] Pirate attacks on modern shipping usually goes unreported because an attacked ship will have to divert its course to file a report in the process delaying the delivery of the ship's cargo. Insurance premiums on attacked ships can also make transportation by ship more expensive for shipping companies because of reduced profits. Finally, ships attacked by pirates run the risk of losing business. Security convoys for shipping companies can range from $20,000 to $100,000, these figures are solely for the Strait of Malacca.[lxxvi] The straits of Malacca alone has 50,000 ships passing through it every year.[lxxvii]

LIVING THE PIRATE CODE

Modern pirates prefer to strike vessels carrying cargo that is easily sold while using the most minimal amount of man power. Today's pirates work in crews of five or less on fast boats that are usually heavily armed. Ships transporting electronic goods are huge magnets for pirates today. Pirates are also known to attack ships simply to hold a ship's crew for ransom. Modern pirates will usually attack a modern ship once it is isolated and pirates typically do so using two boats. The first boat will be carrying the pirate crew for boarding a

LIVING THE PIRATE CODE

ship and the second boat will carry the pirate crew leaders for giving the boarding pirates orders.[lxxviii]

Pirate crews today also survey ships arriving at ports and then pass their information on to other pirates. When a ship is poorly secured by a ship crew, modern pirates simply go on board and steal cargo or whatever they can get their hands on.[lxxix]

It is not unusual for pirates to have informants or pirate crew members working on ships they intend to attack. Informants provide pirate crews with information about the type of cargo being carried by a ship as well as a ship's travel and departure plans. Through informants, modern pirates plan their attacks on unsuspecting ships in order to avoid capture.[lxxx] The ships most vulnerable to attacks by modern pirates roam the waters near Somalia, Nigeria, Tanzania, West Africa, the Red Sea, Bangladesh, Brazil, and the Strait of Malacca between Malaysia and Indonesia.

LIVING THE PIRATE CODE

Holding a ship crew hostage can bring pirates up to $50,000.[lxxxi] Losses to piracy on the high seas total at least 10 billion dollars each year from the most conservative of estimates. Some modern day pirates operate by taking ships and renaming them for resale. The corruption afforded by poverty in developing nations provides pirates with the chance to re-register stolen ships in landlocked nations like Panama, Bolivia, and Mongolia. Modern day pirates need shareholders to finance things such as a ship, boat crew, and light arms including machine guns and rocket-propelled grenades (RPG's). It is believed that larger crime organizations are behind this practice since it takes a good deal of social connections to steal a ship and re-sell it as the process can cost up to $300,000. Ships can also be salvaged in order to sell stolen parts on the black market.[lxxxii] Pirates today, unlike their historic counterparts, may have little experience as sailors. Modern pirates depend on light weaponry, fast boats, and violent crew members that can quickly capture a ship without hurting the cargo or crew members. The emphasis on modern piracy is using the proceeds to benefit other nefarious criminal activities. Modern pirates are primarily motivated to begin their criminal activities because of poverty or private debts with criminal organizations. Unlike pirates in the Golden Age (1650-1730), officers on modern-day pirate vessels are usually chosen by leaders in criminal organizations.[lxxiii] Piracy in Africa is an issue that has been closely monitored by international agencies due to the increase of frequency of pirate attacks affecting international trade. Nigerian pirates concentrate on kidnapping workers in the oil industry. The pirates are motivated by the fact that workers in a specialized field such as operating oil rigs, cannot be easily replaced, and this makes the Nigerian coast among those most frequented by pirates.[lxxiv]

LIVING THE PIRATE CODE

ENGLISH CIVIL LAW & STATUTE LAW IN RELATION TO PIRACY

A pirate is a common enemy with whom neither faith nor Oath is to he kept.

And by the Laws of Nature, Princes and States are responsible for their neglect, if they do not provide security to prevent robberies

Though Pirates are called common Enemies, yet they are properly not that which the term denotes. If Letters of Marque be granted to a Merchant, and instead of taking the Goods or Ships of that Nation from whom their Commission is awarded, take the ship and goods of a friend, this is piracy. And if the ship arrives in any Port of his nation's Dominions, it will be seized and forever lost to the owners, but they are no way liable to make satisfaction.

If a ship is assaulted and taken by the pirates, for redemption of which, the Master becomes a slave to the Captors, by the Law Marine, the Ship and Lading are tacitly obliged for his Redemption by a general Contribution but if it happens through his own Folly, then no Contribution is to be made.

If he be in Enmity with the Crown of England, and are an English pirate in Company with English, and a robbery is committed and they are taken, it is Felony in the English, but not in the stranger for it was no piracy in them, but the depredation of an Enemy, and they will be tried by a Martial Law.

LIVING THE PIRATE CODE

If Piracy is committed by Subjects in enmity with England, upon the British Seas, it is properly only punishable by the Crown of England, who has regimen & dominion exclusive of all other power. If Piracy be committed on the Ocean, and the Pirates be overcome, the Captors may, without any Solemnity of Condemnation hang them up at the next fort.

If Merchandise be delivered to a Master to carry to one Port, and he carries it to another, and sells and disposes of it, this is not Felony, but if, after unloading it at the first Port, he retakes it, it is Piracy.

LIVING THE PIRATE CODE

If a Pirate attacks a Ship, and the Master for Redemption and gives his Oath to pay a Sum of Money, though there be nothing taken, yet it is Piracy by the Law Marine.

If a Ship is riding at Anchor, and the Mariners all aboard and a Pirate attacks her, and robs her, this is Piracy.

If a Man commits piracy upon the Subjects of any Prince or Republic, (though in Amity with us,) and brings the goods into England, and sells them in a Market, the same shall bind, and the Owners are forever excluded.

If a Pirate enters a Port of this Kingdom, and robs a Ship at Anchor there, it is not Piracy, but is Robbery at common Law.

LIVING THE PIRATE CODE

Persons urged by Necessity for taking Cables, Ropes, Anchors or Sails cut off from another Ship that may spare them, they may either pay ready Money, or Money worth for them, or give a Bill for the Payment thereof.

If any natural horn Subjects or Denizens of England, commit Piracy or any act of hostility against his Majesty's Subjects at Sea, under Color of a Commission or Authority from any foreign Prince or State, such offenders shall be judged as pirates.

If any Commander or Master of a Ship or Seaman or Mariner give up his Ship to a Pirate or combine to yield up or run away with any Ship or lay violent Hand on his Commander y or endeavour to make a Revolt in the Ship, he shall be adjudged a Pirate.

LIVING THE PIRATE CODE

All Persons who after the fifth of September 1720,

shall set forth any Pirate (or be aiding and assisting

to any such Pirate committing Piracy on Land or

Sea), shall conceal such Pirates or receive any Vessel

or Goods piratically taken, shall be judged an

accessory to such Piracy and shall suffer.

All Persons who have committed or shall commit

any Offences for which they ought to be judged

with Piracy, may be tried for every such Offence in

such Manner as by is directed for the Trial of

Pirates ; and will not have the Benefit of Clergy,

Shall not extend to Persons conceived or

attainted in Scotland.

This Act shall extend to his Majesty's Dominions in

America, and be taken as a public act.

LIVING THE PIRATE CODE

INDEX

NOTES

_____

_____

_____

_____

_____

_____

_____

_____

_____

_____

_____

_____

_____

_____

_____

_____

LIVING THE PIRATE CODE

NOTES

_____

_____

_____

_____

_____

_____

_____

_____

_____

_____

_____

_____

_____

_____

_____

_____

_____

_____

LIVING THE PIRATE CODE

NOTES

_____

_____

_____

_____

_____

_____

_____

_____

_____

_____

_____

_____

_____

_____

_____

_____

LIVING THE PIRATE CODE

NOTES

_____

_____

_____

_____

_____

_____

_____

_____

_____

_____

_____

_____

_____

_____

_____

_____

_____

LIVING THE PIRATE CODE

NOTES

_____

_____

_____

_____

_____

_____

_____

_____

_____

_____

_____

_____

_____

_____

_____

_____

_____

_____

LIVING THE PIRATE CODE

NOTES

_____

_____

_____

_____

_____

_____

_____

_____

_____

_____

_____

_____

_____

_____

_____

_____

_____

NOTES

_____

_____

_____

_____

_____

_____

_____

_____

_____

_____

_____

_____

_____

_____

_____

_____

_____

_____

LIVING THE PIRATE CODE

NOTES

_____

_____

_____

_____

_____

_____

_____

_____

_____

_____

_____

_____

_____

_____

_____

_____

_____

FOOTNOTES

---

[i] The Seafarers the pirates, pg 22
[ii] Outlaws of the Ocean, pg 285
[iii] Ibid, pgs 285-286
[iv] Ibid pg 286
[v] Ibid 286
[vi] Pirates in History, pgs 1-3
[vii] Ibid, pgs, 6-8
[viii] Ibid, 8
[ix] Ibid 8-10
[x] Ibid pg 4&6
[xi] Ibid pgs 15&16
[xii] Ibid 18
[xiii] Ibid, 17&20
[xiv] Ibid, 22-23
[xv] Ibid, pgs20-21
[xvi] Ibid, pgs 25-26
[xvii] Ibid pg 29&31
[xviii] Pirates of the easterb seas, Ag course, pg 144.
[xix] Under the Black Flag David Cordingly, pg 75
[xx] A.G. Course pg, 141
[xxi] Ibid, pg 76
[xxii] A.G. Course, 142
[xxiii] A.G. Course pgs. 140-141
[xxiv] David Cordingly, pg 76
[xxv] ibid, 78
[xxvi] Ibid, 76
[xxvii] A.G. Course, pg 153
[xxviii] David Cordingly, pg 76
[xxix] A.G. Course, pg 142-43
[xxx] Ibid, 144 and 146, 153
[xxxi] Ibid, 145.
[xxxii] Ibid, 150 and 152 -154
[xxxiii] Pirates Predators of the sea, pg 211

LIVING THE PIRATE CODE

[xxxiv] A.G. Course, 148-149
[xxxv] David, Cordingly, pg 78
[xxxvi] Angus Konstam pirates of, pg 211
[xxxvii] David cordingly, ?
[xxxviii] Frank Sherry, pgs 267-268.
[xxxix] ibid, pg 270
[xl] ibid pgs 272-273
[xli] Rebels and Raiders Frank sherry, pgs 62-63 and 141-142
[xlii] Ibid, pg 54
[xliii] Ibid, pg 58
[xliv] Ibid, pg 123
[xlv] Ibid, pg 129
[xlvi] Blood and Silver, pgs 11-13
[xlvii] Frank sherry, pg 95
[xlviii] Ibid, pg 132
[xlix] Ibid pg 132
[l] The Seafarers the Pirates, Botting pg 50
[li] Ibid pg 24 and 57-58.
[lii] Frank sherry, pgs 136-137 and 139.
[liii] Seafarers, pg 90
[liv] Blood and Silver, pg 111
[lv] Raiders and Rebels, Frank Sherry pg 59
[lvi] Blood and Silver, pg 112- 113
[lvii] Ibid, 111-113
[lviii] Ibid, pg 114
[lix] Ibid, pg 116
[lx] Ibid, pg 117-118
[lxi] Ibid, 119
[lxii] Ibid, 120-122
[lxiii] Rebels, pg 60
[lxiv] Ibid, 122-125
[lxv] Rebels and Raiders, Frank sherry, pg 60
[lxvi] The History of Piracy, Phillip Gosse pg 160
[lxvii] The republic of pirates. pg 74
[lxviii] Ibid, 74
[lxix] Ibid, 70
[lxx] Idiot's guide to pirates, pg 100

[lxxi] Republic of pirates, 74-77

[lxxii] Idiot's guide, 101

[lxxiii] Ibid pg 75-77

[lxxiv] Terror on the High Seas, pg23

[lxxv] Modern day piracy, pg 5

[lxxvi] Terror, pg 34

[lxxvii] modern. pg 24

[lxxviii] Modern, pg 11

[lxxix] ibid, pg 13

[lxxx] ibid, pg 24

[lxxxi] Terror, pgs 23 and 25

[lxxxii] Ibid, pgs 80, 82, 102-104, 110 and 236.

[lxxxiii] Modern, pg 9-10

[lxxxiv] Ibid, pgs 96-97

MIKAZUKI PUBLISHING HOUSE TITLES
25 Principles of Martial Arts©
Arctic Black Gold©
Art of War by Sun Tzu©
Basketball Team Play Design Book©
Beginner's Magicians Manual©
California's Next Century 2.0 by Marcus Ruiz Evans©
Captain Bligh's Voyage©
Coming to America Handbook©
Customer Sales Organizer©
DIY Comic Book: Do It Yourself Comic Book©
DIY Comic Book Part II©
Find the Ideal Husband©
Football Play Design Book©
Freakshow Los Angeles by Carl Crew©
George Washington's Farewell Address©
Hagakure by Hiroki Shima©
I Dream in Haiku by German Sanchez©
IRA Manual of Guerrilla Warfare©
Japan History Coloring Book©
John Locke's 2nd Treatise on Civil Government©
Karate 360©
Learning Magic©
Living the Pirate Code; Story of the World's Greatest Pirates©
Magic as Science and Religion©
Magicians Coloring Book©
Master Password Organizer Handbook©
Mikazuki Jujitsu Manual; Learn Jujitsu©
Mikazuki Political Science Manual©
MMA Coloring Book; Mixed Martial Arts Coloring Book©
Palloncino©
Political Advertising Manual©
Rappers Rhyme Book – Lyricists Notebook©
Self-Examination Diary©
Shogun X the Last Immortal Comic Book©
Small Arms & Deep Pockets©
Stories of a Street Performer©

LIVING THE PIRATE CODE

Storyboard Book©
Swords & Sails; The Legacy of the Red Lion by D. McAvoy©
Tao Te Ching©
The Adventures of Sherlock Holmes by Sir Arthur Conan Doyle©
The Book of Five Rings by Miyamoto Musashi©
The Bribe Vibe©
The Card Party©
The History of Acid Tripping: How LSD Changed America©
The Medium Writer by Terry Allen Dodson©
Tokiwa: A Japanese Love Story©
T-Shirt Design Book©
United Nations Charter©
Words of King Darius©
World War Water©

EDUCATION IS THE KEY TO HAPPINESS©
www.MikazukiPublishingHouse.com©

www.ingramcontent.com/pod-product-compliance
Lightning Source LLC
Chambersburg PA
CBHW031556040426
42452CB00006B/322